THIS BOOK

BELONGS TO

....

1. **LOOK CAREFULLY AT THE PICTURES**

2. **TRY TO DRAW THE SAME**

GOOD LUCK!

YOUR TURN

YOUR TURN

YOUR TURN

YOUR TURN

YOUR TURN

YOUR TURN

YOUR TURN

YOUR TURN

YOUR TURN

YOUR TURN

YOUR TURN

YOUR TURN

YOUR TURN

YOUR TURN

YOUR TURN

YOUR TURN

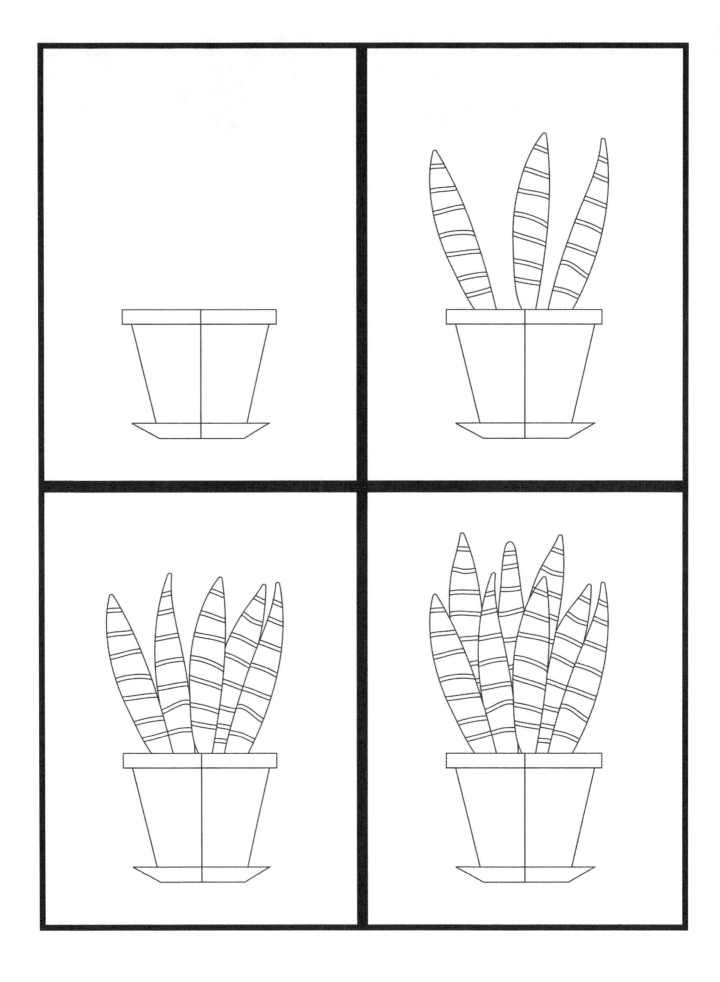

YOUR TURN

YOUR TURN

YOUR TURN

YOUR TURN

YOUR TURN

YOUR TURN

If you liked it please give us review.

Made in the USA
Coppell, TX
01 July 2023

18671718R00026